The Busy Mom's Book of

QUICK
CRAFTS

for Kids

The Busy Mom's Book of
QUICK CRAFTS
for Kids

Judith Logan Lehne

Illustrated by Tracey Wood

STERLING PUBLISHING CO., INC.
NEW YORK

Edited by Hazel Chan
Design by Carol Thompson

Library of Congress Cataloging-in-Publication Data

Lehne, Judith Logan.
  The busy mom's book of quick crafts for kids / Judith Logan Lehne—[Rev. ed.]
    p. cm.
  Rev. ed. of: The never-be-bored book. 1992.
  Includes bibliographical references and index.
  ISBN 1-4027-1547-1
  1. Handicraft–Juvenile literature. I. Lehne, Judith Logan. Never-be-bored book. II. Title.
TT160.L443 2004
745.5–dc22
                                                    2004006475

10 9 8 7 6 5 4 3 2 1

Published by Sterling Publishing Co., Inc.
387 Park Avenue South, New York, NY 10016
© 2004 by Judith Logan Lehne
Originally published under the title *The Never-Be-Bored Book:*
  Quick Things to Make When There's Nothing to Do
© 1992 by Judith Logan Lehne
Distributed in Canada by Sterling Publishing
% Canadian Manda Group, 165 Dufferin Street
Toronto, Ontario, Canada M6K 3H6
Distributed in Great Britain and Europe by Chris Lloyd at Orca Book
Services, Stanley House, Fleets Lane, Poole BH15 3AJ, England
Distributed in Australia by Capricorn Link (Australia) Pty. Ltd.
P.O. Box 704, Windsor, NSW 2756, Australia

Manufactured in the United States of America
All rights reserved

Sterling ISBN 1-4027-1547-1 Hardcover
             1-4027-1952-3 Paperback

To my children, Shane, Kyle, Todd, and Tessa, for sharing their imagination and creativity with me as I wrote this book, and to my grandchildren, Brendan and Elijah, for giving me an excuse to play no matter how old I get. May the spirit of childhood always be alive in your hearts.

CONTENTS

Introduction

Preparations

Crafts Quick to Please

Projects with Style

Recipe File

Acknowledgments

About the Author

Index

Introduction

You say you're bored with baseball on a hot summer day?
You say the autumn wind has blown the blahs your way?
You say the springtime rain has dampened all your fun?
And winter feels like it'll last until you're twenty-one?
Say no more! Don't whine and cry!
Boredom's a thing of the past!
With imagination and a few supplies,
you can still have a blast!

It's every busy mom's dilemma: engaging with your child in activities that are fun, creative, and educational. Whether you're looking for a way to get rid of the "nothing-to-do's," or need a gift for a friend, or a project idea for your child's school, you'll find just what you need in this book. These projects are not "busywork"— the kinds of things you and your child make and then throw away. Each activity allows both of you to create real artwork and things you can use every day. Your child can also get a chance to learn about different cultures since he or she will be making replicas of traditional objects, artwork, and musical instruments. He can also engage in simple scientific experiments. But, most of all, he'll have a terrific time.

Some projects require the use of sharp knives or a hot stove, so it may be best for you to read through the

steps of the project first and then do the more dangerous parts while your child watches. You'll find the easier, quick projects—which take from minutes to one day—in the first section of the book. More complicated projects are in the second section. But don't let your child shy away from these more difficult crafts. His patience will be rewarded with a wonderful finished product. The final section contains "recipes" that are needed for making the items that will be used for some of the crafts.

This book also includes projects that your child can sell at arts and crafts fairs or garage sales. And, of course, he can make lovely, inexpensive gifts for friends, family, and teachers. Most materials for these craft projects can be found in nature or in your own home. You can buy other materials for very little. So, close the door on your child's boredom and open him up to the magic world of creativity and imagination.

Judith Logan Lehne

Preparations

*I*n each of the projects, the needed materials are listed in a box. Most of them can be found in nature or around the house. Others can be found at arts and crafts shops, variety stores, or hardware stores.

What to Do

• Decide with your child which project she would like to do. Check that you have all the materials necessary.

• Projects that require the use of stoves, ovens, knives, or sharp tools have a HOT! or SHARP! symbol before the directions. Read over the instructions carefully beforehand. You should do the step(s) in which a hot or sharp item is used.

HOT!   **SHARP!**

• Protect your work surface with newspapers or plastic.

• Have fun with your child as you do the project.

Crafts Quick to Please

MAKE THEM WITH EASE

Dream Catchers

You'll Need
- Forked twig
  (*green*, not dry)
- 2 to 3 yards (1.8
  to 2.7 m) of yarn
  or string
- White liquid glue
- Feathers or
  beads
- Scissors

These pretty homemade webs are adapted from Native American culture. According to Native Indian lore, if a child hangs a Dream Catcher over the bed, the web will "catch" the bad dreams and let the good dreams through. The next time your child has a nightmare, maybe you can help him make one.

DIRECTIONS

1. Bring the forked ends of the twig together and wind the yarn, or string, in a crisscross way to hold the ends in place. Knot the yarn and let 4 to 6 inches (10 to 15 cm) of yarn hang down.

2. Begin where you've tied the twig branches together. Tie four separate pieces of yarn across the opening of the twig branches to create a wheel-spoke pattern. Knot each end of yarn as you work.

3. As you draw the fourth piece of yarn across the opening, wind the strand around the yarns at the center once or twice. Then pull the strand to the other side and knot it.

4. Snip off the excess yarn ends close to each knot.

5. Put several drops of glue on each crossed strand so that you create a spiral of glue dots.

6. With a long piece of yarn, set the yarn onto each glue spot, connecting the dots until you've created a "web." Press each spot with your finger to help the yarn strands adhere to each other.

7. When the glue is dry, attach beads or feathers to the hanging strands of yarn at the bottom of the Dream Catcher.

8. Make a yarn bow at the top. Add more beads, if you wish.

9. Hang the Dream Catcher over your child's bed. Sweet dreams for him!

Hullabaloo Kazoo

The Kazoos are so quick and easy to make. You and your child can create several. Then have her invite her friends over to form a Hullabaloo Kazoo Band.

You'll Need
- 6-inch (15 cm) cardboard tube
- 4-inch (10 cm) square of cellophane or waxed paper
- Rubber band
- Medley of tunes

DIRECTIONS

1. Cut a cardboard tube so that it is 6 inches (15 cm) long, or use an empty toilet tissue role.
2. Spread the cellophane or waxed paper square over one end of the tube. (Do not use plastic wrap.)
3. Secure the paper with a rubber band.

4.«Decorate the kazoo with nontoxic paint or decals, if you wish. Just avoid painting the mouthpiece.

Have your child place the open end of the tube against his mouth, then hum. She may have to experiment with different mouth positions before the kazoo will distort the sound of her voice.

You'll Need

- Small jar
- Moth flakes, glitter, or crayon shavings
- Water
- Waterproof glue
- Small plastic or glass figures

Blizzard in a Jar

Imagine snow swirling around tiny trees, miniature animals, or soldiers—even on a hot summer day. With a few materials, you and your child can create a snowstorm to keep in his room all year long.

DIRECTIONS

1. Glue the glass or plastic figures to the inside bottom of the jar. Allow them to dry for 24 hours.
2. Fill the jar with water, leaving a ½-inch (1.3 cm) space at the top.
3. Add 2 tablespoons of moth flakes for white snow. Or you can make snow in different colors with glitter or crayon shavings.
4. Coat the rim of the lid with glue. Screw the lid on the jar, and allow the glue to dry.

Shake the jar and turn it upside down. When you turn the jar upright, you and your child will see a blizzard.

Paper Fortune-Teller

With a quick lesson in paper folding, your child will soon be able to "predict" the future for her friends. Or she'll be able to create a Smile-Maker that coaxes everyone to smile.

You'll Need
• 8½-inch (21.6 cm) square of white paper
• Pen or pencil
• Pocketful of dreams

PAPER FOLDING

1. With the paper square flat, fold all four corners in so that they meet at the center. You may use a larger or smaller square of paper, but this 8½-inch (21.6 cm) square works nicely.

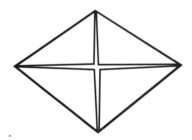

2. Turn the paper over, and again fold corners to meet in the center.

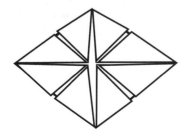

3. Turn the paper over again, and fold it in half, **corner to corner**. Reopen it.

4. Fold the other two corners together.

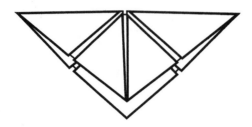

5. Reopen the paper form with the four square flaps up.

6. Stick your index fingers and thumbs under the four flaps, and move the Paper Fortune-Teller back and forth and side to side.

TELLING FORTUNES

1. Write the numbers on the different parts of the flaps as shown in the illustration. The predictions go beneath the inside flaps. (See step 6 illustration.) For ideas on what kind of predictions to write, see "Some Fortunate Predictions," page 24.

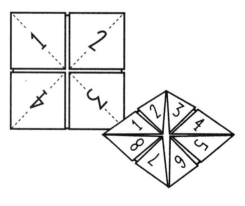

2. Fold the Paper Fortune-Teller again so that you can place your fingers under the flaps. Ask your child to pick one of the four numbers that are showing.

3. Work the Paper Fortune-Teller back and forth and side to side while counting to the chosen number. Make one movement for each count.

4. Now ask your child to choose a number from the eight numbers showing inside the Paper Fortune-Teller. Again move the Paper Fortune-Teller while counting the chosen number.

5. Ask your child to pick a number from the ones that can now be seen inside.

6. Lift the flap, and read the prediction written under that number.

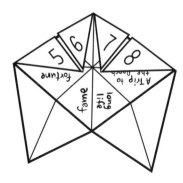

7. Now that your child knows how to use the Paper Fortune-Teller, have her predict the future for her friends.

SOME FORTUNATE PREDICTIONS

You and your child can have fun writing your own predictions. Or try some of these traditional ones.

"You'll soon have money."

"You'll soon have a special reason to smile."

"One day you'll be famous."

"You'll find something you have lost."

"A wish will come true."

"You'll live a long time."

SMILE-MAKERS

Fill in the spaces for predictions with something that will make your child smile: "You are special," "Love your smile," or even simply "Boo!" You can call these Paper Fortune-Tellers "Smile-Makers." Your child can give it to a best friend or a brother or sister.

Roller Printing

This is a great way to make lots of prints quickly!

DIRECTIONS

Before beginning, cover the work surface with newspapers or plastic to protect it from stains.

With Soup Can Rollers, designs can be larger and you can include several different designs on one can. These large roller printers are easy for your child's small hands to use.

SOUP CAN ROLLER

1. Use an *unopened* soup can. You don't need to remove the label.
2. Cut small shapes from the cardboard and glue them around the can. Or, you can dip the string or rubber bands into the glue and wind them around the can.
3. Allow the glue to dry.
4. Brush paint on the shapes or on the string. You could also use a stamp pad.
5. Have your child roll the soup can across the paper he chose.

You'll Need
- Stamp Pad (see page 130)
- Paper for printing (plain note paper, white tissue paper, brown grocery bags, or construction paper)
- Scissors
- Cardboard paper

Soup Can Roller
- Soup can
- White liquid glue
- Scissors
- Cardboard paper
- Several pieces of string, 12 to 18 inches (30½ to 46 cm) long *or* one or more large rubber bands
- Paint and brush

Carrot Roller
- Fat carrot
- Peeler
- Paring knife
- Two toothpicks
- Plate
- Plastic food-wrap
- Food coloring *or* paint and brush

* * *   * * *

CARROT ROLLER

Creating designs on carrot rollers takes great care and patience, since the surface area of the carrot is a relatively small space. But the designs will be delicate and produce natural, artistic results when you print them.

CAUTION: Steps 1 to 3 require the use of a sharp instrument. It is recommended that you do these steps rather than your child.

1. Find a fat carrot and peel it.
2. Cut a 3-inch (7.6 cm) piece from the carrot. This piece should be fairly uniform in diameter.
3. With a paring knife, cut shapes and designs all around the carrot.
4. Have your child place a toothpick at each end.
5. Put several drops of food coloring (see page 133) or natural dye (see page 126) on a plate covered with plastic wrap and roll the carrot across the food coloring. Or you can brush the carrot with paint, or even use a stamp pad (see page 130).
6. Let your child roll the carrot across the paper he chose.

ROLLER-PRINT DESIGNS

•Your child can roll her printer across sheets of tissue paper or uncrinkled grocery bags to make original gift wrappings.

•She can also roll her printer across note paper or folded typing paper to make special note cards for herself or for a friend.

•Frame the roller-print pictures your child made on construction paper.

•And here's an idea: use fabric paints (see page 132) and help your child roll designs across a T-shirt. After the fabric paint dries, he'll have a one-of-a-kind shirt.

Magic Spectacles

Looking at the world through rosy red glasses can be wacky, wild fun for you and your child. Make these Magic Spectacles and discover all kinds of funny and interesting surprises that await the two of you. You can also use these Magic Spectacles to teach your child about primary (red, blue, and yellow) and secondary (purple, green, and orange) colors. Have her look at the blue sky through the lenses. Ask her what happens.

DIRECTONS

1. On poster board or heavy paper, draw two circles, each about 3 inches (7.6 cm) in diameter.

2. Inside each circle, draw another circle, leaving ½ inch (1.3 cm) all the way around.

3. Carefully cut out the smaller, inside circles.

4. From a piece of red cellophane, cut two 3-inch (7.6 cm) circles. If you cannot find any red cellophane, use clear cellophane or plastic wrap. Simply color the cellophane or wrap with a permanent red felt-tip marker.

5. Glue the cellophane circles to the poster-board circles.

6. Glue the inner circles to a Popsicle stick.

7. Wait until the glue dries, then look through the glasses to see a magical rosy world.

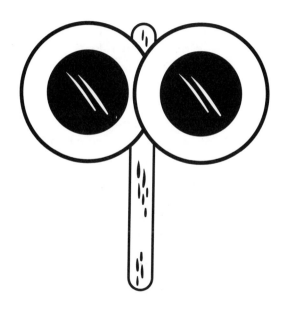

Flying Butterfly

These colorful paper butterflies make cute hanging decorations for your child's room, but they can also be used for active play.

DIRECTIONS

1. Fold the construction paper in half.
2. Draw a butterfly wing pattern on the paper as shown.
3. Cut around the pattern lines, but do not cut the fold.
4. Unfold and decorate the wings with assorted scraps of construction paper, if desired.
5. Slide the butterfly's wings between the clothespin opening and glue them to the clothespin.
6. Cut antennae from construction paper slightly longer than you wish them to be. Make a small fold at the bottom of each antenna and glue it to the head of the clothespin.
7. Cut two pieces of thread, each about 30 inches (76 cm) long.
8. Tie one end of one piece of thread around the head of the clothespin, and knot, making the knot side on top.
9. Tie the other thread around the bottom of clothespin, about ½ inch (1.3 cm)

from the bottom. Leave the knot side up.

10. Allowing the butterfly to hang free, gather both threads together 12 to 18 inches (30½ to 46 cm) from the base. Adjust the threads so that the butterfly is balanced as it hangs, and make a knot in the two threads.

11. Gather the threads at the top and make a loop or another knot.

12. Using a thumbtack, fix the looped end of thread to the ceiling of your child's room. Now the butterfly is ready to fly! Your child can also make the butterfly "fly" indoors or

outside by carefully holding the top end of the thread and making the wings flap.

You'll Need

- Clip-type clothespin
- 2 sheets of 8½ x 11 inch (21.6 x 27.9 cm) construction paper
- Colored cellophane or tissue paper
- Scissors
- White liquid glue
- Bright acrylic paint or nail polish

Stained-Glass Butterflies

Open your child to the world of stained glass by creating these imitation stained-glass paper butterflies. They produce a similar effect and are very easy to make. Afterwards, you may follow up this project with a trip to your local antique store.

DIRECTIONS

1. Place the two sheets of construction paper on top of each other. Fold them in half.
2. Draw a wing pattern on the folded construction paper as shown.
3. Cut out the wings, but do not cut along the fold.
4. With the construction paper still folded together, make another small fold along the top of the wing. Then cut a random-shaped hole in the small folded area.
5. Repeat this several times, making holes along the wing from top to bottom. Be careful so that the holes don't overlap.
6. Open up the wings, and set aside one of the wing patterns.
7. Cut a piece of colored cellophane (or tissue paper) to fit over one of the

wings without allowing the edge to overlap. Repeat for the other wing.

8. Glue cellophane to the wings.

9. Smear glue all around the wings, avoiding the hole areas.

10. Place the second wing pattern on top of the first with the cellophane sandwiched in the middle. Line up the patterns carefully so that the holes match. Then press the two construction paper wings together and allow the glue to dry.

11. Glue the middle section of the butterfly to one flat side of the clip clothespin. Let the butterfly dry.

12. After it dries, clip your butterfly where light will shine through. Window-shade pulls and curtain edges are nice spots for Stained-Glass Butterflies to rest. Or you could clip

You'll Need

- Large piece of plastic, old plastic table-cloth, or plastic place mat(s)
- Can of inexpensive shaving cream (enough for two children)
- Food coloring or watercolors
- Smock or old shirt to protect clothing
- Spoons, Popsicle sticks, and other assorted items

Shaving-Cream Sculptures

This is something that you and your child can get your hands into! If you do this on a summer day, then the both of you can quickly clean the picnic table off with a garden hose.

DIRECTIONS

1. Cover the work area with plastic.
2. Cover yourself and your child with a smock.
3. Spray a large mound of shaving cream in front of each of you. Remind your child that this is *not* whipped cream, so don't eat it!
4. Use the spoon and other implements you've assembled to poke, scoop, and plop the shaving cream. For example, the two of you can decide to each make a dog; see how your creations turn out.
5. Place one or two drops of food coloring on the mounds. Then make finger-paint designs. Experiment with color combinations, like yellow and blue, red and blue, or yellow and red. Have your child guess what color he will get before mixing them.
6. You can also make funny beards and moustaches on your own faces. Be careful that your child does not get any

shaving cream into his eyes—it stings! If your child wants to pretend to shave, have him use a spoon handle or Popsicle stick. Don't let the shaving cream stay on your faces for a long time. Wipe it off carefully with a damp cloth.

7. When you're finished sculpting, use paper towels to scoop the remaining shaving cream into a trash can. Rinse your hands in a sink or tub, then wipe off the plastic covering on the work area with a damp cloth.

Jack Frost Suncatchers

You'll Need
- Pie plate or cake pan
- Berries, flower blossoms, or snips from evergreen branches
- Long string or yarn
- Water

These delightful outdoor ornaments can be made year-round and kept in the freezer until Jack Frost settles in for the winter.

DIRECTIONS

1. Fill a pie plate or cake pan with water.

2. Carefully lay the string or yarn on top of the water around the edge of the pan. Let the ends of the yarn hang over the outside of the pan. (Leave enough yarn to tie the suncatcher to a tree when you've completed it.)

3. Arrange colorful berries, bits of pine branches, snips of flower blossoms, coils of apple peel, and other natural objects in the pan.

4. Place the pan in the freezer until the entire pan of water is frozen solid. (Make sure the pan sits flat.)

5. When Jack Frost arrives, and the temperature outside remains below 32°F (0°C), hang the suncatcher in a tree with your child. Enjoy its shimmer as the winter wind plays upon the suncatcher. For warm seasons, store the suncatcher in a plastic bag and keep it in the freezer until Jack Frost appears.

MORE IDEAS

•Add a few drops of food coloring to the water before freezing it to get a stained-glass effect from the suncatcher.

•Include birdseed with the berries and flower petals. When the temperature rises and the suncatcher begins to melt, birds will be able to peck through the ice for a snack.

Ghost-a-Notes

Help your child become an amateur detective or supersleuth by sending her Ghost-a-Notes.

DIRECTIONS

1. Fill the pan with water.

2. Put one sheet of paper into the pan. When the paper is completely wet, *carefully* remove it and place it on a flat surface.

3. Wet the second sheet of paper and place it on top of the first sheet.

4. With the ballpoint pen, write a message on the top sheet. Discard the top sheet after you've finished writing.

5. Allow the bottom sheet to dry completely. When it is dry, you won't be able to see the writing—*until* the paper is wet again!

IDEAS FOR GHOST-A-NOTES

- Have your child make a April Fools' Day card for her Dad. Make a real, *visible* design on the outside of the card, but let her do her "ghost writing" inside.

- Use Ghost-a-Notes for birthday invitations. Use the ghost writing for the time, place, and name of the guest of honor.

• Your child can write a mystery story for her friends to read but use ghost writing for the important clues.

NOTE: Remember to include visible writing to explain how to get the invisible message to appear: "To read the secret message, wet the paper!"

Hobbyhorse Puppet

Create a special pony friend for your child or a corral full of characters for his own puppet show.

You'll Need

- Old sock with heel
- Old nylons, panty-hose, socks, or stuffing material
- 12-inch long (30½ cm) wooden dowel or sturdy twig
- Assorted rubber bands
- White liquid glue
- Felt-tipped markers
- Yarn
- 4-inch (10 cm) square of card-board
- Scissors

DIRECTIONS

1. Have your child fill an old sock with stuffing material, or use old nylons or socks to stuff it. Fill the sock from toe to heel and just beyond. Leave 3 to 4 inches (7.6 to 10 cm) of the cuff unstuffed.

2. Insert a dowel or straight twig into the sock with the heel side up. Wrap a rubber band tightly around the outside of the cuff to hold the dowel in place. For added security, add some glue on the dowel inside the sock.

3. To make the horse's ears, grab up a little of the sock at the heel stitchings, then wrap each ear with small rubber bands.

4. Use felt-tip markers to make the horse's eyes, nose, and mouth.

5. Using about 7 yards (6.4 m) of yarn, wind it around the 4-inch (10 cm) cardboard square, letting both ends hang loose at the bottom.

6. While holding the yarn in place at the top of the cardboard, cut the yarn across the bottom.

7. Position the yarn on the horse's head to form the mane. Glue or stitch the yarn into place.

8. Cut a few strands of yarn and position the strands on the horse's head so that it falls around the eyes. Glue or stitch the yarn strands in place.

You'll Need

- 8 ½ x 11-inch (21.6 x 27.9 cm) paper
- Scissors
- Felt-tip markers, crayons, or colored pencils
- White liquid glue
- Glitter

Floating Angels

This is a variation on a chain of paper dolls. This is a great craft to do during Christmas. Your child can decorate these angels and use them as a tabletop Christmas display.

DIRECTONS

1. Fold the paper in half along the width and cut along the fold into two 4¼ x 11-inch (10.8 x 27.9 cm) strips. (Reserve one strip for another set of angels.)

2. Fold the strip in half as shown. Then fold the strip the same way two more times.

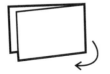

3. Copy the angel pattern onto the paper.

4. Cut all around the outline *except* at the ends of the wings and the skirt.

5. Open out the folded angels. Let your child draw faces, hair, and other details on the backs and fronts of the angels.

6. For fancy angels, spread a drop of white glue on the wings and halo. Then sprinkle them with glitter.

7. Stand the angels on a smooth surface, like a table, and have your child blow gently toward it. The paper angel will "float" across the surface!

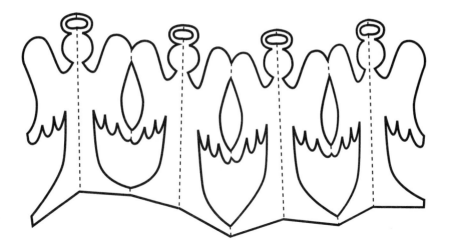

* * * * * * * *

Pinecone Flowers

Pinecone Flowers are great to put into a pretty vase. Gather different pinecones by taking a walk outside with your child. He can learn about the many trees they come from.

DIRECTONS

1. Cut the top off a pinecone, leaving the flower shape at the bottom.

2. To make the stem, use a dried twig with narrow branches that form a "V" at the top. Trim the twig to suit the stem length you desire. Trim the "V" branches so that the pinecone stem fits between them.

NOTE: If you cannot find V-shaped twigs, substitute brown pipe cleaners. Add 2 inches (5 cm) to make the desired stem length. Wrap one pipe cleaner end around the pinecone's base.

3. Put glue on the "V" branches and fit them around the stem—or if there is no stem, the base of the pinecone.

4. Allow the glue to dry.

Necklace-Face Folks

Necklace-face folks are sure to help curb your child's boredom when she takes them with her on long car trips.

DIRECTONS

1. Have your child draw the profile of a person's head with only its eyes.
2. Make a hole in the poster board at the top of the head and another hole where the chin and neck meet.
3. Pull one end of the chain or cord through the top hole, from the front of the picture to the back, and tape ½ inch (1.3 cm) of chain on the back of the profile. Repeat at the bottom hole with the other end of the chain or cord.
4. Gently push the chain around to create the forehead, nose, lips, and chin. Your child can give each folk a very funny face. She can also try out different profiles.

MORE IDEAS

For additional fun, have your child draw an animal's body and attach the chain so that she can create unusual animal heads. Imagine a cat's body with the head of a horse or a horse's body with a pig's head!

You'll Need

- A clean, white 100% cotton dish towel (*not* terry cloth)
- Crayons
- Newspapers
- Iron

Crayon Batik

Batik is a Javanese word that means "wax painting." This method of creating designs with dyes and wax was first used by ancient Asian tribes in 3000 B.C. It was brought to Europe by Dutch traders in the 17th century. Ancient batik designs required many different materials and much time. With this crayon batik project, you and your child can create batik-like designs quickly and easily.

DIRECTIONS **hot**

1. With the towel right-side up, have your child place his left hand on the towel's bottom left side. Let him trace around his hand with a crayon.

helping hands

2. On the towel's bottom right side, a little higher than the tracing of his left hand, have your child trace with a crayon around his right hand.

3. Below his handprints, have him neatly write the words "Helping Hands" with a crayon.

4. Now take a crayon and go back over all your crayon designs to make sure the colors and outlines are vivid.

5. Heat an iron to the cotton setting.

6. Place a thick layer of newspapers on the ironing board.

7. Place the towel crayon-side down on the newspapers.

CAUTION: Steps 8 and 9 require the use of a hot iron. It is recommended that you do these steps rather than your child.

8. Press the towel with the hot iron for several minutes, moving the iron over the design area. Be careful not to scorch the fabric!

9. Remove the newspapers carefully and replace them with another layer of newspapers. Press the towel again.

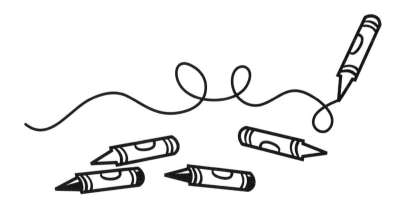

10. Let the towel cool completely and remove the newspapers. Now your child is ready to lend a helping hand in the kitchen.

MORE IDEAS

•This method can be used to create designs on T-shirts, too.

•Launder crayon batik towels and T-shirts in cool water to retain their bright colors.

•Your child can also create his own original designs on canvas tennis shoes. After he has drawn designs on his tennis shoes, tightly stuff the shoes with wadded newspapers. Then place newspapers on top of the crayon designs and iron. Remove the iron from the surface of the newspapers frequently to prevent the paper from burning.

Bookmark Corners

These handy bookmarks are so easy to make, you and your child can create several for all her schoolbooks.

SEWING PROJECT

1. Fold the felt square in half diagonally, matching corners neatly.
2. Cut along the fold to make two identical triangles.
3. Pin the triangles together. If your child wants to do this step, be careful that she does not accidentally stick herself with the pins.
4. Sew along the two 3-inch (7.6 cm) edges with a running stitch or an overcast stitch. Use a thread color that contrasts with the color of the felt.
5. Knot the thread at the end of the second 3-inch (7.6 cm) edge and remove the pins.

GLUING PROJECT

1. Using construction paper instead of felt, follow the directions for the sewing project.

You'll Need
- 3-inch (7.6 cm) square of felt or construction paper
- Scissors
- Pearl-head pins
- Needle and thread *or* glue

2. Glue the 3-inch (7.6 cm) edges together. Use the glue sparingly since you only want to glue the very outer edges of the bookmark.

3. Allow the glue to dry before using your bookmark.

MORE IDEAS

•Slip the open end of the bookmark over the top corner of the page your child wishes to mark.

•If your child wants to decorate the bookmark corners, she can use glue and glitter or sew on sequins. But if she uses glue, be sure that it's completely dry before placing the corner on a book page.

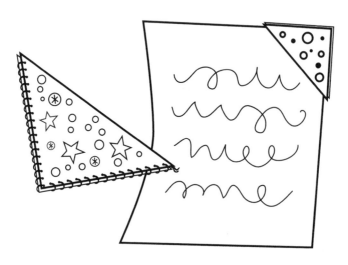

Block Printing

Block printing is an ancient art that is practiced in Europe, Asia, and North and South America. Native American tribes used block prints to decorate their tools and clothing, and they sometimes created block-print designs on their bodies for special occasions. Native Americans used various objects from nature to create these printing blocks. You and your child can spend a rainy afternoon creating unique letter paper, note cards, or gift wrap with your own printing blocks made from natural or household objects.

DIRECTIONS

1. If your child wants to use objects from nature, have him collect them. Be careful not to damage the plants and trees. Let him clean off any dirt or loose particles.

CAUTION: Step 2 requires the use of a sharp instrument. It is recommended that you do this step rather than your child.

2. If your child wants to use items from around the house, collect and prepare them for printing. Coil and tie the belt. Make a clean cut at one end of the

You'll Need

- Objects from nature: leaves, twigs banded together and cut evenly at one end, acorn caps, rocks with bumps and ridges
- Things from around the house: glass with a raised design, an old leather belt coiled and tied, celery and carrot slices, potatoes with carved-out designs
- String, glue, wood block, or small cardboard box for a string printer
- Watercolor paint, acrylic paint, or natural dye (see pages 126, 132–134)
- Stamp Pad (see page 130)
- Assorted paper

celery or carrot. Slice the rounded end from the potato and carve a design. The raised portion of the potato design will print.

3. If your child chooses to use a string printer, add white glue to create a swirly, twisty design on the wood block or the bottom of the cardboard box. Have him lay the string carefully on the glue design, and allow it to dry completely.

4. To print, press the object to be printed onto the stamp pad. Make sure that all of the design is covered with paint.

5. Firmly press the printer (potato, acorn, or whatever you choose to print) onto the paper, then lift the printer carefully.

6. Repeat steps 4 and 5 until he finishes the design he wants on his paper.

7. Allow the printed paper to dry thoroughly.

* * * * * * * *

Eggshell Art

Mosaic art dates back to ancient times. Ancient Egyptians made mosaic jewelry and decorated furniture from pieces of glass and stone. In India, marble mosaics adorn the outside of some buildings, and caskets and kitchen utensils were often decorated with materials such as wood, ivory, and shells. You and your child can create mosaics with this Eggshell Art activity. You can use the leftover shells from breakfast eggs or dyed Easter eggs.

> **You'll Need**
> •Eggshells in various colors
> •White liquid glue
> •6-inch (15 cm) square of cardboard or thin plywood
> •Clear acrylic spray

DIRECTIONS

1. Break up the eggshells into pieces no smaller than ½ inch (1.3 cm).
2. If you are using the leftover peelings from hard-boiled Easter eggs, the coloring has already been done. If you are using white eggshells from breakfast, you'll need to color the shells.
   a. Collect several small bowls or cups. Place ½ cup (120 ml) of water in each. Add ½ teaspoon (2.5 ml) of vinegar and several drops of food coloring in each bowl. Use one color for each bowl of water. Or, if you wish, dye the shells with natural dyes (see page 126).

b. Place the broken shells in the bowls of food coloring and allow them to stand for ½ hour. Remove the shells and place them on paper towels to dry.

3. Spread white liquid glue on the cardboard or plywood, working in one small area at a time. Select pieces of eggshell and press them gently onto the glue. Arrange the shell pieces in a pattern, design, or picture.

4. Continue gluing eggshells to the cardboard or plywood until the entire surface is covered with shells. Allow the glue to dry.

5. Spray the finished design with a clear acrylic coating and allow the paper to dry.

6. Glue a strong picture hanger to the back of the cardboard or plywood. Or use self-adhesive hangers. You can hang your child's Eggshell Art masterpiece in her room.

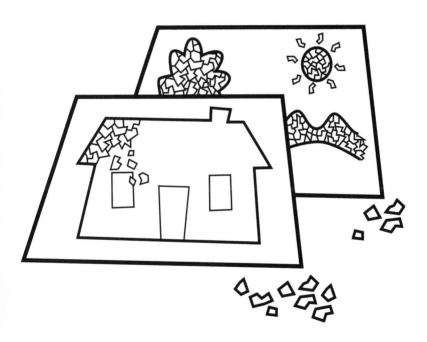

You'll Need

- Sugar Cookies (see recipe on page 120)
- 18 Popsicle sticks
- 1 or 2 baking sheets
- Rolling pin
- Small juice glass
- Fast & Fabulous Frosting Glaze (see recipe on page 124)
- Assorted sprinkles, colored sugar, or small candy pieces

Lollipop Cookies

These cookies are great to have for your child's next birthday party, or any other occasion. They are fun to make, plus they are something that the two of you can sink your teeth into!

DIRECTIONS hot

1. Mix the cookie dough for the Sugar Cookies. Wrap the dough in plastic, and refrigerate it at least 1 hour.

2. Sprinkle flour over the rolling surface. With a rolling pin, roll out the dough until it is about ¼-inch (0.6 cm) thick. Use a small juice glass to cut out circles of dough.

3. Place one of the dough circles on a baking sheet.

4. Place one Popsicle stick on top of the dough circle, about halfway up the middle.

5. Place another circle of dough on top of the first one on the cookie sheet. Have your child press lightly all around the circle to blend the two pieces of dough together.

6. Continue to do the same thing with the rest of the cookie dough circles. Leave a 1-inch (2½ cm) space between each Lollipop Cookie and its Popsicle stick.

7. Bake the cookies in a preheated oven at 375°F (190°C) for 10 to 12 minutes. Immediately remove the cookies from the baking sheet, and let them cool slightly.

8. To decorate the cookies, make a batch of frosting glaze (see page 124).

9. With a flat knife or spatula, spread a little frosting on top of a cookie. Quickly—before the frosting hardens—add sprinkles, colored sugar, or small pieces of candy. Set them aside for your child's party. But, of course, both of you should also have an early taste.

MORE IDEAS

•You can make Halloween cookie pops. Simply color your frosting orange, and add candy corn for jack-o'-lantern faces. Or how about Valentine pops? Use heart-shaped cookie cutters and pink frosting. For Easter you could decorate egg-shaped cookies.

•Dough for drop cookies can also be baked lollipop-style. See Chocolate Drop Pop recipe on page 122.

Crafts Quick to Please

Sand-Castle Candles

A sand-castle candle is a fun thing to make after a trip to the beach. Be sure that you do not leave the candle in your child's room where she may light it on her own. Keep it in a family room so that the two of you can enjoy it whenever you reminisce about the trip.

DIRECTIONS

1. Fill shoe box with damp sand.
2. Have your child use her fist or a glass to make a hole in the center of the sand. Don't let the hole go all the way to the bottom of the shoe box.
3. With her finger, poke four tunnels at least 1 inch (2½ cm) deep at the bottom of the hole. Make sure that the tunnels connect to the hole and that they are spaced evenly around the hole. These tunnels will serve as the "feet" for the candle.
4. Wrap the candle wick around a pencil or Popsicle stick, and let one end fall to the bottom of the sand castle's hole. Position the pencil on top of the box so that the wick remains straight.

CAUTION: Step 5 requires the use of a lit candle. It is recommended that you do this step rather than your child.

5. Melt the candle wax. Slowly pour the melted wax into the hole.

6. When the wax hardens, pull out the candle and brush off excess sand.

7. Set the candle on a heat-proof plate to protect the table or other surface it rests on.

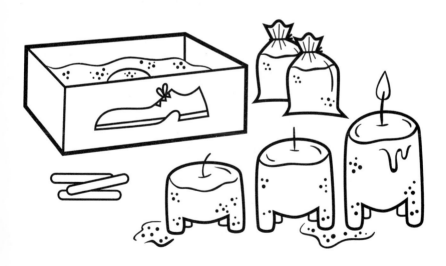

You'll Need
- Shiny magazine paper (*not* a magazine cover)
- Scissors
- Sponge

Paper Snakes

Water is one of the main ingredients in making paper. When paper mills process magazine paper, much of the water is squeezed out to form the sheets. When the paper comes in contact with water again, it reacts in curious ways. You can show your child the ways paper reacts to moisture, and also have fun when the two of you make these paper snakes.

DIRECTIONS

1. Cut a wiggly-snake shape from a page of shiny magazine paper. Cut a length of snake from the outside paper edge *toward the opposite edge.*
2. Saturate a sponge with water and set it on a plate.
3. Place the snake, shiniest side up, on the sponge.
4. Watch carefully! As the paper absorbs moisture from the sponge, the snake will coil and dance.
5. If you allow the paper snake to dry completely, you can use it over and over again.

* * * * * * *

Yarn Flowers

You and your child can enjoy pretty blossoms made from brightly-colored yarn year-round.

DIRECTIONS

1. Place an 8-inch (20.3 cm) piece of yarn along the length of the marker. Have your child hold the yarn firmly in place with his thumb and forefinger.

2. Use the same color of yarn to wrap the first yarn strand around the diameter of the marker twenty times, leaving 4 to 5 inches (10 to 12.7 cm) of yarn at each end.

You'll Need
- Scraps of yarn in several colors
- Large marker with a ¾-inch (1.9 cm) diameter or larger base
- 8-inch (20.3 cm) green pipe cleaners
- 5-inch (12.7 cm) green pipe cleaners

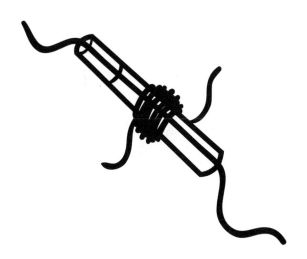

3. Hold the marker so that all four yarn ends fall in the same direction.

4. Place the marker on the work surface, and tie a knot in the ends.

5. Hold the resulting yarn flower at the top, and carefully remove it from the marker.

6. Work an 8–inch (20.3 cm) pipe cleaner through the loop at the bottom of the flower. Bend the pipe cleaner, then twist it to form the flower's stem.

✳ ✳ ✳ ✳   ✳ ✳ ✳ ✳

7. Separate the yarn loops to create the flower petals.

8. Make the leaves by bending 5-inch (12.7 cm) pipe cleaners into a "V" shape, then twist the open ends together around the stem. Shape the leaf however you wish.

9. Repeat steps 1 to 8 to make more flowers in many colors.

You'll Need

- Soap Snow (see recipe on page 118)
- Beads, buttons, and small candies for decoration
- Ribbon or strip of scrap fabric
- Black construction paper
- Empty thread spool
- Black paint or black marker
- White liquid glue
- Paper plate

Summer Snowman

You don't need a blustery cold day or a thigh-high snowfall to make these all-weather snow sculptures.

DIRECTIONS

1. Whip up a bowl of Soap Snow (see page 118).
2. Wet your hands and your child's hands to keep the snow from sticking to them.

3. Pack the snow into three snowballs—one large, one medium, and one small.
4. On the paper plate, stack the balls on top of each other in size order, with the largest on the bottom.
5. Using assorted beads, buttons, and candies, give the snowman eyes, a nose, and a mouth.
6. Tie a ribbon or fabric strip around the snowman's neck.
7. For the snowman's hat, use the paint or marker to color the spool black.
8. For the rim of the snowman's hat, cut a circle a little larger than the spool's diameter out of black construction paper.
9. Glue the circle to one end of the spool.
10. Place the hat on the snowman's head.

For more ideas on what to do with Soap Snow, see the Recipe File, page 118.

* * * * * * * *

You'll Need

- 3 x 8½-inch (7.6 x 21.6 cm) felt
- Scissors or pinking shears
- Ruler
- Needle and thread
- Iron
- Permanent felt-tipped marker
- Glue and sequins or glitter

Tooth-Fairy Pockets

These handy holders will keep baby teeth safe under a pillow or on a nightstand until the Tooth Fairy can collect them—and perhaps leave a shiny coin in their place!

DIRECTIONS **hot**

1. With the pinking shears, pink the top 3-inch (7.6 cm) edge of the felt. Or use scissors to make a scalloped edge.
2. Measure 3½ inches (8.9 cm) up from the bottom, and fold it up toward the top of the felt.

CAUTION: Step 3 requires the use of a sewing needle. It is recommended that you do this step rather than your child. Or, your child can use fabric glue to join the two sides of the felt instead.

3. Beginning at one of the top corners, sew the overlapping pieces of felt together using a running stitch or an overcast stitch. Sew around both sides and the bottom. Your child can also use fabric glue instead of sewing the two sides of felt.
4. Fold the top scalloped edge over the sewn pocket. This will be the back of the pocket.

5. Press lightly with a hot iron. (You should also probably do this step.)

6. On the front side of the pocket, have your child print her name in the possessive with a permanent marker. Below that, print the word "tooth." (For example: Mary's tooth.)

7. If she wishes, help her decorate her Tooth-Fairy Pocket with sequins and glitter. Then, when she loses a tooth, she'll have somewhere to keep it, or she can put it under her pillow for the Tooth Fairy.

You'll Need

- Medium to large pinecones
- 18-inch (46 cm) piece of cord or ribbon
- Recipe for Crunchy Creature Stew (see page 125)
- Newspapers or a bowl

Pinecone Creature Feeders

These pretty feeders hold and hide an edible treat for feathered and furry creatures alike. After you hang them outside, you and your child will soon see wildlife in your backyard.

DIRECTIONS hot

1. Tie one end of the ribbon or cord around the upper part of a pinecone—about 1 to 2 inches (2½ to 5 cm) from the top. Tightly tie and knot the cord.
2. Make a slip knot at the top end of cord.
3. Make some Crunchy Creature Stew (see page 125). Since this recipe requires a stove or microwave, it is recommended that you prepare the stew rather than your child.
4. Hold the pinecone at an angle over newspapers or a bowl. Drip globs of hot stew onto the pinecone "petals." As it

cools, the stew will become thick.

5. When the pinecone is nicely filled, hang your feeder from a tree branch or a hook near a window. That way, you and your child will be able to watch your visitors enjoy their treat.

MORE IDEAS

•Make more feeders to hang in your yard.

•Try adding different ingredients to your Crunchy Creature Stew recipe to see what kinds of critters you attract.

Projects with Style
BUT THEY TAKE AWHILE

You'll Need
- A can of white Play-Doh, or homemade Flour Dough, Salt Dough, or Cornstarch Clay (see recipes on pages 112—117)
- Small scraps of fabric
- Whole walnuts, unshelled
- Heavy thread, yarn, or 1/16-inch (0.6 cm) ribbon
- White liquid glue
- Cotton balls
- Fine-line black felt-tip marker

Mouse in a Cradle

This small sleeping mouse makes a cute Christmas tree decoration or tie-on for wrapping gifts for your child's friends. The little fellow will also be quite comfortable rocking from a window-shade pull or from a decorative hook in your child's room.

DIRECTIONS **hot**

1. Carefully crack and shell the walnuts. Do not break the halves. Each cleaned-out half shell will make one cradle.

2. Roll a little modeling dough into a ball the size of a large pea. This will be the mouse's head. Take half that amount for each ear. Roll the dough into two small balls, then flatten each. Carefully press the ears onto the head.

3. Attach the entire head to a piece of dough $\frac{1}{2}$ to 1 inch (1.3 to $2\frac{1}{2}$ cm) long. Since you won't be able to see the body when the project is finished, you need not be fussy about the shape. Just make sure the mouse's body is not too long to fit into the cradle.

4. Put the mouse in a place to dry. This will take several days. If you want to speed up this part, put the mouse on a foil-lined cookie sheet, and bake it for 1 to 2 hours at 250°F (121°C). Allow it to cool and dry for at least 24 hours.

5. Draw a face on the mouse's head with the marker—sleeping eyes, a nose, and whiskers.

6. Using half of the walnut shell, place a little cotton inside to make a "pillow" for your mouse. Glue the cotton to the shell.

7. Glue the mouse to the cotton.

8. Cut a small square of fabric of about $1\frac{1}{2}$ inches (3.8 cm) for the cradle blanket. Tuck the blanket around the sleeping mouse, up to his "chin." Glue it in place, using a few drops of glue on the mouse and the shell.

9. Cut two pieces of thread or narrow ribbon 8 inches (20 cm) long. Glue one ribbon lengthwise underneath the shell, allowing both cut ends to meet under the shell.

10. Repeat this with the second ribbon, gluing the second ribbon around the shell's width.

11. Gather the two ribbons together at the top of the shell so that the cradle hangs evenly. Glue the ribbons together at the top, or use a small piece of ribbon or thread to tie them together.

12. Find a special place in your child's room, or somewhere else in the house, for this quiet little mouse.

Tin-Punch Pictures

Tinware has been used at least since the Bronze Age, because bronze is an alloy of copper and tin. Tinplate art was developed in Mexico in about 1650 when Spain restricted the availability of silver. And since tin was so inexpensive, it was commonly used by smiths and craftspeople in 18th- and 19th-century Europe and America as a substitute for silver and pewter.

It is easy and inexpensive to use old tin-punch techniques to make lovely new pictures. You can find tinplate at craft or hardware stores. And some old local newspapers still use it. You might be able to buy some from your hometown paper.

You'll Need
- Sheet of tinplate
- Scissors
- Hammer
- Nails
- Pattern for your design
- Cardboard, several sizes larger than your tinplate piece
- Masking tape
- Felt-tip marker
- Tracing paper
- Ruler
- Paper towels
- Window cleaner
- Picture frame

DIRECTIONS

1. Decide with your child what size she wants her picture to be. A good size to start with is 5 x 7 inches (12.7 x 18 cm), since it easily fits into an inexpensive frame.

2. Choose a pattern. Find a picture with a simple design. Preschool coloring books often have large, easy pictures that make great patterns. You can also find

patterns in cross-stitch books and stencil-design books. Be sure the design fits inside the picture-frame size you've chosen.

3. If the pattern your child wants to use is from a library book, she can copy the design on tracing paper. Make sure she keeps a steady hand while she traces the pattern with a pencil. Or, if the design is on a loose sheet, you could make a photocopy. If it's OK to tear the pattern from a coloring book, tear it out carefully, and you're ready to go!

4. With a felt-tip marker, make *evenly spaced* dots around the outlines of the pattern. This will take patience, but it is important to space the dots just far enough apart so that each punch you make with a nail will be separate, but close to, the rest.

CAUTION: Step 5 deals with sharp edges. It is recommended that you do this step rather than your child.

5. Cut the tinplate to the picture size you've chosen. Use your ruler, measure carefully, then cut with scissors. Be careful: The edges of cut tin can be very sharp!

6. If the tinplate came from a newspaper, clean the back (where the printing is) with a paper towel and alcohol or window cleaner.

7. Use masking tape to tape the tinplate—shiny side up—to the board.

8. Carefully center the design, then tape the pattern over the tinplate.

9. Have your child place a nail on one black dot of the pattern while you lightly tap it with a hammer. You will not have to

pound hard, since tinplate is thin and you only want a small hole for each pattern dot.

10. Continue punching around the dots of your design until you punch in all the holes. Carefully lift one end of the pattern to make sure you haven't missed any dots. When you've finished, untape the pattern from the tin.

11. Remove the punched tin from the board, and carefully wipe it with a towel and window cleaner to remove any smudges.

12. Frame the finished picture, but do not cover it with glass. You could make a window ornament from the punched picture by gluing ribbon around the raw edges of the tin and tying a ribbon from the top. Sunlight will stream through the holes.

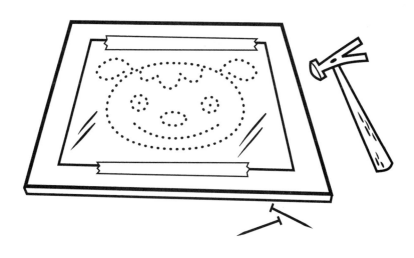

You'll Need

- Flowers picked on a dry, sunny day—remove all but 1 inch (2½ cm) of the stem
- 24-ounce (672 g) box of yellow cornmeal or 3 cups (720 ml) of sand
- 1 cup (240 ml) of uniodized salt (iodized salt is OK, but flower colors will fade slightly)
- Shoe box with lid
- Sheets of waxed paper or paper towels
- Watercolor brush
- Wire stems
- Acrylic spray or hair spray (optional)

Dried Flowers

Before you and your child begin to gather your favorite flowers for drying, here are some guidelines.

- Handle flowers that you want to dry with care. Use a sharp knife or scissors to cut the flower several inches down the stem. Don't pull the flowers from the ground since this can damage their root system.

- Keep all flowers you collect in water until you can process them. This will keep the blossoms fresh.

- It's best to process the flowers as soon as you can after picking to help preserve their natural colors.

CORNMEAL AGENT

1. Collect flowers that are in full bloom. Only roses should be picked *before* they are in full bloom, since they continue to open during the drying process.

2. Strip all leaves from the flower's stem, except one or two leaves near the blossom. If you prefer to have no leaves, that's fine.

3. Mix the cornmeal and the salt thoroughly to create your agent.

4. Line the shoebox with waxed paper or paper towels.

5. Cover the bottom of the container with ½ inch (1.3 cm) of the agent—the cornmeal and salt mixture.

6. Place the flowers on top of the agent; leave at least 1 inch (2½ cm) between blossoms. Place larger flowers facedown and smaller ones faceup.

7. Use a teaspoon to add small amounts of the agent to the flower. Sprinkle the agent in and around the petals so that it covers the entire flower. Work on one flower at a time.

8. Dry just a single layer of flowers in one container.

9. Cover the container with the lid and allow the flowers to dry for 4 to 6 days. The larger the flower, the longer it will take to dry. Do not overdry. This will cause the petals to be brittle and to break easily.

10. Have your child check to see if the flowers are dry by gently pushing his finger through the agent; the petals should feel like thin paper. When the flowers are dry, carefully shake

the box over a bowl or cookie sheet to remove the agent. Save the cornmeal-salt agent since you can use it again.

11. Gently push the agent away from the blossoms with your fingers. If any cornmeal-salt sticks to the flower, gently brush it off the petals with a small watercolor paintbrush.

12. Insert a wire stem into the piece of stem that you left on the flower. Be careful not to push the wire through the top of the blossom. If you want to add a little shine to your flower, spray it lightly with acrylic spray or hair spray.

13. Make a bouquet of dried flowers, and place it in a vase to enjoy long after summer flowers have disappeared from gardens.

SAND AGENT

You can substitute sand for the cornmeal, since sand and salt also make an effective agent for preserving dried flowers. Simply use 3 cups (720 ml) of sand to 1 cup (240 ml) of salt.

Rhythm Sticks

Long ago, Native Americans made rhythmic music by rubbing two specially crafted sticks together. These rhythm sticks were called *guayos*. Your child can make his own rhythm sticks, similar to those made by the Native Americans.

DIRECTIONS

1. Let your child decide which side of the large dowel or branch he wants to be the rhythm stick's top. If he is using a tree branch, help him remove the bark and any twig sections.

CAUTION: Step 2 requires the use of a sharp knife. It is recommended that you do this step rather than your child.

2. Cut notches along the rhythm stick's top, spacing these notches ¼ inch (0.6 cm) apart. Leave a 4-inch (10 cm) section unnotched at the end of the stick for the handle.

3. If you use a twig for the top rubbing stick, peel off any bark, and sand the twig until it is smooth. If you use a dowel for the rubbing stick, you're ready to make music.

You'll Need
- Dowel or tree branch, 18 inches (46 cm) long and 1 to 2 inches (2½ to 5 cm) in diameter
- Dowel or sturdy twig, 12 to 14 inches (30½ to 35½ cm) long and ½ inch (1.3 cm) in diameter
- Sandpaper
- Large, dried gourd (optional)
- Sharp knife

To play the Rhythm Sticks, rub the smooth, narrower stick across the notches in the wider stick. Turn on the radio or pop a CD into the CD player, and begin to create various rhythms to accompany the music.

To make the sound from the rhythm stick louder, place the stick on a large, dried gourd; then rub the smooth stick across the notches. The hollow gourd will amplify the sound and make it easier to hear your music.

Your child can personalize his *guayos* by drawing designs on them with permanent markers. Or, if you know someone with wood-burning tools, perhaps he or she would be willing to engrave your child's name or a design on the rhythm sticks for him.

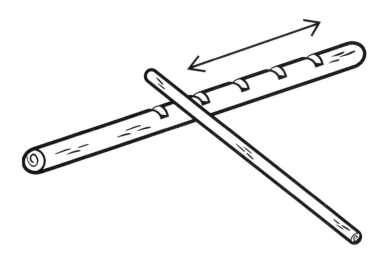

☆ ☆ ☆ ☆ ☆ ☆ ☆ ☆

Spatter-Dyed Toy Bag

This can be a messy project. So work outdoors, in the basement, or in the bathroom, where spills will be less of a problem. Wear rubber gloves, if you have them, and old clothes.

DIRECTIONS

1. Spread newspapers on the work surface.

2. Spread plastic on top of the newspaper.

3. Lay a dry pillowcase on top of the plastic. Place a piece of plastic inside the pillowcase, and smooth the pillowcase so that it lies flat.

4. With a food-coloring bottle, you and your child can sprinkle, splash, and dot color randomly on the pillowcase.

5. Repeat step 4 with all three remaining colors.

6. Using a spray bottle, wet the pillowcase with water. As the pillowcase gets wet, the colors will begin to merge and blend. Avoid drenching the pillowcase with water, but make sure the entire surface is damp.

7. Carefully turn over the pillowcase, and repeat steps 1 to 6 on the other side.

8. Pin the pillowcase at its corners to a hanger, and hang it up to dry. Since the

You'll Need
- White pillowcase
- Food coloring
- Spray bottle filled with water
- 2 large plastic bags or sheets
- Newspapers
- Cord or ribbon 36 to 40 inches (91 to 102 cm) long
- Scissors or hole-punch
- ½ cup (120 ml) vinegar
- ½ cup (120 ml) water
- 3 tablespoons (45 ml) salt

pillowcase will drip as it dries, be sure to protect the area under the pillowcase with newspapers or plastic.

9. When the pillowcase is *completely dry,* it's a good idea to set the colors. Soak the bag for ½ hour in a solution of ½ cup (120 ml) of vinegar, ½ cup (120 ml) of water, and 3 tablespoons (45 ml) of salt. Then allow the bag to dry again.

NOTE: If you want to wash the bag, wait at least 48 hours after it has completely dried. Then wash it separately.

10. Use a pencil or black marker to mark along the pillowcase's entire hem. Space dots 2 inches (5 cm) apart and 2 inches (5 cm) away from the pillowcase's open end.

CAUTION: Step 11 may require the use of sharp scissors. It is recommended that you do this step rather than your child.

11. With sharp scissors or a hole-punch, poke holes all the way through the pillowcase at each marked dot. You could sew buttonholes around each hole, but it isn't necessary.

12. Work the narrow cord or ribbon through the holes, beginning with one of the middle front holes and ending with the other middle front hole.

13. Make a big knot in each end of the cord; this will keep the cord from slipping back through the holes. To close your toy bag, pull both ends of the cord at the same time.

MORE IDEAS

• If your child has an old white T-shirt that's stained, you can use this spatter-dyeing method. That way, stains will seem to disappear and she'll be able to wear her wild and wacky shirt.

• To create a wild, WOW! outfit, splatter-paint a pair of painter's white overalls with fabric paint. Your child can wear them with one of her "designed-it-myself" T-shirts.

☆ ☆ ☆ ☆ ☆ ☆ ☆ ☆

• The best way to "paint" a T-shirt, of course, is with fabric paints made specially for this purpose. Also, they don't come off in the wash.

HURRY-UP METHOD

If your child is more interested in the finished product than in the creative process, use ready-to-use fabric paints (see page 132). They will be more reliable in producing consistent results.

Simply splatter the fabric paints onto the pillowcase, then roll up or fold the pillowcase to blend and merge the colors. You'll greatly reduce processing and drying time with this method.

Clay Dolls

With some patience and time, you and your child can create a one-of-a-kind doll. This four-part project should not be rushed. So, gather the materials and be sure to read *all* the directions before beginning. You can even help your child celebrate important people from history by sewing a costume for a pirate, Viking, explorer, Native American, cowboy, or ancient queen.

SCULPTING **hot**

1. Make Cornstarch Clay according to the recipe on page 116.
2. Using the clay, sculpt the head and shoulders as one unit. (See below illustration). For support, push a toothpick or thin nail through the center of the head to the shoulder section. Cover the hole made by the nail at the top of the head with clay.

You'll Need

Sculpting
- Cornstarch Clay (see recipe on page 116)
- Toothpicks
- Assorted carpenter nails
- Sharp pencil
- Aluminum foil
- Shortening
- Baking sheet

Painting
- Acrylic paints
- Cottonballs, yarn, or furry fabric
- Clear acrylic spray

Creating the Doll's Body
- White liquid glue
- Large sheets of plain paper
- Cotton fabric, in a solid color
- Quilt stuffing or old nylons
- Needle and thread (sewing machine)
- Safety pins
  continued

continued

- Heavy hand-sewing needle
- Heavy thread (buttonhole twist or carpet thread)

Dressing the Doll
- Plain paper
- Assorted clothing fabric
- Needle and thread (sewing machine)

3. Create the doll's face—eyes, nose, mouth, and ears—by carving them with a toothpick, sharp pencil, or fingernail. Carefully work the clay to form cheeks, chin, forehead, and eyebrows, if your child want lots of definition.

4. Hollow out the shoulder section, and poke holes into the front and back of the shoulders with a carpenter's nail (see step 2 illustration). Since these holes will be used to attach the body to the doll, be sure they will allow a needle and thread to pass through.

5. Mold feet and hands, making them extra long so that you can glue on the arm and leg sections later. If necessary, use toothpicks for extra support.

6. Cover a baking sheet with lightly greased foil.

7. Crumple a small piece of foil to fill the shoulder cavity and support the head section. If possible, place the torso upright on the baking sheet. Otherwise, lay it down faceup. Also place the doll's feet and hands on the baking sheet.

8. Bake them at 200°F (95°C) for 2 to 3 hours. Let all doll parts cool and dry completely—at least 24 hours.

PAINTING

1. Use acrylic paints to color in the doll's face, eyes, mouth, hands, and feet or shoes. Allow the paint to dry.

2. To preserve the painted doll, spray all the clay parts with clear acrylic spray. Apply two light coats, and allow each coat to dry completely.

3. Use cotton balls, yarn, or scraps of a furry fabric to glue hair, eyebrows, or even a beard to your doll.

CREATING THE CLOTH BODY

1. Draw a pattern on plain paper for the doll's body. Make the pattern outline about 1 inch (2½ cm) larger than the finished body. The pattern can be the same for both boy and girl dolls.

2. Cut two identical pattern pieces out of cotton fabric.

3. With right sides together, stitch around the outline of the fabric pieces. Leave the arm, leg, and shoulder openings unstitched. Turn the finished garment right-side out.

4. Pin the arm and leg openings closed with safety pins, and stuff the body until it becomes quite firm.

5. Remove pins from the openings, and gently push the clay leg and arm pieces into place. Glue the doll's arms and legs to the fabric, and allow them to dry.

6. Glue the shoulder and head unit to the fabric in the same way.

7. Use strong thread—like buttonhole twist or carpet thread—and a needle to attach the fabric through the holes in shoulder piece. (You should probably do this step.)

DRESSING THE DOLL

1. Using the paper pattern for a guide, make more patterns for shirts, pants, or a dress. Remember that the clothes must fit over the doll's stuffed body, so your clothing patterns must be at least 1½ inches (3.8 cm) larger than the original pattern for the doll's body.

2. Cut patterns from any fabric your child likes. Sew the clothing by hand or by machine. Felt and polyester fabrics are easy to work with since their raw edges do not fray.

3. After you help the doll into his or her outfit, you are done. Remember that the finished doll will be fragile, so handle it with care. Your child can place it on a doll stand to display it safely.

NOTE: You may be able to find ready-made doll clothes that fit your child's doll. Also, some fabrics can be glued together, eliminating the need for sewing.

HISTORICAL DOLLS

You can teach your child a little history by helping her make historical dolls. Find a time or place that interests your child. Help her read up on a historical figure from that period: how that person looked, what he or she wore, etc. This is an opportunity to experiment with making beards, unusual hairdos, and replicas of unique historical clothing and accessories.

Dandy Rock Candy

You'll Need
- 1 cup (240 ml) of water
- 4 cups (960 ml) of sugar
- Blue food coloring
- Pint-size (470 ml) canning jar
- Quart-size (1 l) cooking pot or bowl
- String
- Pencil

Although it's quite simple to make candy crystals, it takes some time. Since temperature and humidity will affect the growth of crystals, it could be as long as a couple of weeks to make rock candy, and the size of the final crystals can range from small, pearl-size candy to walnut-size whoppers.

You can make this project a scientific experiment with your child. Through trial and error, keep trying until both of you are happy with the results.

DIRECTIONS hot

CAUTION: Making candy crystals requires the use of a conventional stove or microwave. It is recommended that you do step 1 rather than your child.

1. **For the stove**: pour 1 cup (240 ml) of water into a quart-size pot. Add 2 cups (480 ml) of sugar, and stir over medium heat until the sugar dissolves completely. Do *not* boil. Gradually add the remaining 2 cups (480 ml) of sugar and 2 drops of the blue food coloring. Continue to stir until all the sugar is

completely dissolved. Be careful—you can be badly burned by melted sugar.

For the microwave: place 1 cup (240 ml) of water in a microwavable 1-quart (1 l) bowl. Stir in 2 cups (480 ml) of sugar and microwave for 5 minutes on high. Remove and stir. Be very careful. The bowl and the sugar water will be very hot! Repeat the microwave process until all the sugar is completely dissolved. Stir in the remaining 2 cups (480 ml) of sugar and 2 drops of blue food coloring. Continue to microwave at 3- to 5-minute intervals until all sugar is dissolved.

2. Carefully pour the sugar water into a clean glass jar.

3. Cut the string into three pieces so that each piece is about 12 inches (30½ cm) long.

4. Tie each string around the pencil so that all six ends can hang down into the sugar water when the pencil is placed across the rim of the jar. Do *not* let the strings rest on the bottom of the jar.

☆   ☆   ☆   ☆   ☆   ☆   ☆   ☆

5. Now comes the hard part: waiting. Set the jar some place where it will not be disturbed. About every other day, use a spoon or knife to *gently* break up the crystals which cover the top of the sugar water. But be careful not to stir the water or lift the strings. Just wait. And wait.

6. In about 1 to 2 weeks, your child will have some nice, big sugar crystals, and some yummy rock candy!

☆　☆　☆　☆ ☆　☆　☆　☆

Tin-Punch Lantern

In colonial days, many houses were lit by candles placed in tinplate *lanthorns*, a 16th-century word for "lanterns." Punched holes admit oxygen and allow light to shine through. You and your child can make a simple version of a colonial lanthorn to use as a candleholder.

DIRECTIONS

You'll Need
- Clean 16-ounce (448 g) tin can
- Hammer
- Nail
- Paper pattern for tin-punch design
- Masking tape
- Newspapers or towel

1. Remove the lid and the label from a tin can. (You should probably do this step.)

2. Fill the can with water and freeze it until the water becomes solid ice.

3. Choose your pattern. (See directions for making tin-punch designs on pages 75.) Make a design all the way around the can, or use just one side.

4. Lay the can containing frozen water on its side atop newspapers or a towel.

5. Tape the pattern to the can. Leave a ½-inch (1.3 cm) margin around the bottom of the can. This will prevent melted wax from leaking through the punched holes.

6. Pound a nail into each dot of your pattern on the can. Perhaps your child can hold the nail while you lightly tap it.

☆   ☆   ☆   ☆   ☆   ☆   ☆   ☆

7. When you finish punching in the design, remove the paper pattern and the ice. Put a candle inside the can.

8. Place this candleholder on a heat-proof surface, since the heat from the candle will make the can quite hot.

Enjoy the lovely light designs that flicker from the lanthorn.

☆ ☆ ☆ ☆ ☆ ☆ ☆ ☆

Miniature Maracas

Maracas are percussion instruments that orig-inated in Brazil. Most maracas are made of dried gourds or round rattles with pebbles in them. You and your child can make small maracas out of walnut shells. Afterwards, you can use them to dance to spicy Latin salsa or Latin jazz beats.

You'll Need
- Walnuts
- White liquid glue
- Popsicle sticks
- Small beads, buttons, or seeds
- Paint or nail polish
- Sandpaper or file
- Rubber band

DIRECTIONS

1. Carefully open a walnut so that you have two uncracked halves.
2. Remove everything inside the shells. Save the nutmeats for a quick snack.
3. Sand or file the shell's flat bottom end so that you can insert the Popsicle stick and fit the shell halves together.
4. Place one or a few tiny buttons, dried apple seeds, cherry pits, or small beads inside one half–shell. Avoid crowding the shell so that the maraca will be able to make noise.
5. Drop a little glue on the edge of one shell half.
6. Glue one end of the Popsicle stick.
7. Put both halves of the shell together with the Popsicle stick in between.

8. Wind a rubber band around the shell to hold both halves together tightly until the glue dries. This will take several hours.

9. Your child can decorate the maraca with acrylic paints, or cover it with a clear varnish or nail polish.

MORE IDEAS

Your child can invite some friends over to create a percussion band. With several walnut maraca instruments and one or more Rhythm Sticks (see page 81), everyone will soon be rockin' with the rhythm. Include a few Hullabaloo Kazoos (see page 18) to add strange and wonderful wind-instrument melodies. Your child might even be inspired to compose her own new spicy Latin music.

Burlap Baskets

Baskets made from burlap are lovely alone, but they can also become containers for your child's dried flower or yarn flower creations. And they are wonderful when filled with home-made potpourri (see page 135).

You'll Need
- 12-inch (30½ cm) square of burlap
- White liquid glue
- Large mixing bowl
- Small bowl, rounded glass, or muffin dish with flat bottom
- Clear plastic wrap

DIRECTIONS

1. Cut the burlap into a circle about 11 inches (27.9 cm) in diameter.

2. Place the burlap circle in a large mixing bowl, and squeeze white liquid glue onto the burlap.

3. Thoroughly saturate the burlap with the glue, working the glue into the burlap with your hands. This is gooey work! Wash your hands after the burlap is completely soaked with glue.

4. Wrap plastic wrap around the outside of the small bowl, glass, or muffin dish. Stuff excess plastic wrap inside the bowl or glass.

5. Now, the work gets messy again. Take the gluey, mushy burlap and place it on a flat surface covered with plastic wrap. Place the bowl in the center of the circle of burlap.

☆ ☆ ☆ ☆ ☆ ☆ ☆ ☆

6. Mold the burlap around the bowl. Make a ruffled edge at the top. Use scissors to make the edge even, if necessary. Wash the scissors after you use them or they'll be sticky ever after.

7. Set the basket on a plastic-covered surface to dry.

8. When the burlap is thoroughly dry, remove the small bowl. Wash the bowl in hot water to remove any traces of glue.

9. Tear the plastic wrap out of the burlap basket's inside.

This basket could also be used for party nut cups. You and your child could also make flower arrangements with dried flowers

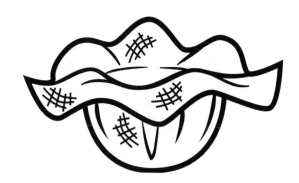

You'll Need

- Tube of refrigerator biscuits
- Aluminum foil
- Cookie sheet
- Clear acrylic spray
- Heavy pot (used as a weight)

Baked Napkin Rings

Napkin rings made from ready-to-use biscuit dough add fun to your child's next party. For extra special occasions, tie a narrow ribbon into a bow around the top of the napkin ring.

CAUTION: These napkin rings are only for decorative purposes. Do not let your child or anyone eat these rings.

DIRECTIONS **hot**

1. Crumple a large piece of aluminum foil into a tube, about 8 to 10 inches (20.3 to 25.4 cm) long and 1½ inches (4 cm) in diameter.

2. Line the cookie sheet with foil.

3. Cut one unbaked biscuit into three equal pieces.

4. Roll each piece of dough into a thin rope.

5. Pinch one end of each rope together. Take turns with your child holding the pinched-together ropes in place.

6. Braid the dough ropes, but leave a small end of each rope unbraided.

7. Carefully wrap the braid loosely around the foil tube to form a circle. Pinch the ends together.

☆   ☆   ☆   ☆      ☆   ☆   ☆   ☆

8. Place the tube on a cookie sheet with the pinched ends of braid on the bottom.

9. Make several braided rings, and place each one on the foil tube, leaving 2 inches (5 cm) between each ring.

10. Bake at 250°F (120°C) for 1 hour.

11. Carefully remove the foil, and allow the dough rings to cool.

12. Place the cooled rings in a dry place for at least 2 days.

13. Cover the work area with newspapers, and spray the bottom and inside of the dough rings with acrylic spray. Allow the rings to dry completely, then spray the top of the rings. Allow the tops to dry.

MORE IDEAS

• A set of four or six napkin rings makes a very nice gift.

• How about making tiny braided rings to be used with scarves, neckerchiefs, and sashes?

You'll Need
- Medium or large green apple
- Lemon juice
- Paring knife
- Pencil
- 2 whole cloves
- Liquid dish detergent bottle and cap
- Sand or dried rice
- Cotton balls or yarn
- 2 squares of 18-inch (46 cm) fabric
- White liquid glue

Apple-Head Doll

Apple carving is an old art, but the results are always surprising. Since the fruit shrinks as it dries, the carvings on the face change, and the doll appears to "age" before your very eyes.

DIRECTIONS

CAUTION: Steps 1 to 3 require the use of a knife. It is recommended that you do these steps rather than your child.

1. Pare the apple. Do this very carefully to remove the skin, but keep the surface as smooth as possible.
2. Remove a small amount of core from the bottom.
3. To carve the face, use a small paring knife. Make deep cuts for the eyes. For the nose, cut wedges on each side for cheeks so that the nose sticks out a bit. Make a slit for the mouth. If you want more detail, you can also sculpt the cheeks and chin by carving away small bits of apple from those areas. But remember, just make *shallow* cuts.
4. Use your fingernail or a straight pin to scrape wrinkles into the forehead, cheek, and chin areas.
5. Soak the apple in lemon juice for 15 minutes.
6. Lightly dry the apple with a paper towel, and insert a pencil at the bottom of the apple, where you removed the core.
7. To dry your apple head, put the pencil into a jar or bottle, making sure that the apple does not touch *anything* as it dries. If anything touches the apple while it dries, that could cause the apple to spoil.
8. Allow 3 to 4 weeks for the apple head to dry.
9. On the *second day* of the drying time, poke whole cloves into the eye holes.
10. On the *sixth day* of the drying time, remove the pencil from the apple head, and place the head on the pull-up cap of a plastic dish-detergent bottle.
11. After the drying time is complete, glue the head to the bottle cap, if necessary.

12. Fill the detergent bottle with sand or dried rice to prevent the doll from tipping over. Screw the cap with the apple head onto bottle.

13. For the Apple-Head Doll's dress, drape fabric around the bottle, with the fabric's raw edges in back. Cut the fabric to fit the bottle, and allow for fullness at the shirttail or the skirt's bottom. Glue the fabric together, then glue it to the back of the bottle.

14. Glue cotton balls or yarn to the doll's head for hair. Allow the glue to dry.

15. Fold the cape fabric in half diagonally, then cut it to the size you want. Be sure to make it long enough to tie.

16. Position the cape on the doll's head, and tie it in front, under the chin. Make sure the tied knot does not leave any of the bottle exposed. Adjust the fabric, and use glue, if necessary.

MORE IDEAS

Each Apple-Head Doll you make will seem to have a personality all its own, depending on the facial features you and your child create and the way the apple dries. You can make an outfit for each doll by experimenting with different fabrics. You could use ruffles to cover the neck instead of a cape.

Wishing Pin

Instead of breaking the wishbone from a roasted chicken or turkey to make a wish come true, leave the wishbone whole and make a good-luck pin that your child can keep handy for months. May all of her wishes come true!

DIRECTIONS

1. Thoroughly wash the wishbone from a turkey or chicken, and allow it to dry for several days.

2. Use acrylic paint or nail polish to paint one side of the wishbone. Allow the paint to dry. Paint the other side.

3. Tie a ribbon around the head of a safety pin, and knot it securely. Add a little glue to the back of the knot.

4. With the glue-side of the knot against the wishbone's neck, tie a ribbon around the other side of the neck. Add a spot of glue between the ribbon and wishbone. Knot the ribbon tightly. Finish with a pretty bow.

You'll Need

- Salt Dough (see recipe on page 114)
- Glasses in assorted sizes
- Objects for creating designs—fork, straw, cookie stamps, things with raised or depressed designs
- Aluminum foil
- Plastic wrap or waxed paper
- Rolling pin
- Cookie sheet
- Ribbon or string
- Beads, glitter, or other decoration

Mosaic Medallions

Shimmery! Sparkly! These mosaic medallions make lovely jewelry or wall plaques for your child.

DIRECTIONS

1. Make Salt Dough according to the recipe on page 114.
2. Place the dough on a piece of aluminum foil.
3. Place plastic wrap or waxed paper on top of the dough, and roll it out to the desired thickness. About ½ inch (1.3 cm) works well for small creations like necklaces. Remove the plastic wrap.
4. Choose a drinking glass the size your child wants her circle to be. Turn it upside down on the dough and press down firmly to cut the dough into a circle. Carefully lift the glass. Make several circles in various sizes.
5. Using the straw, press a hole near the top of the round medallion. Make sure that you remove all the dough from the hole.
6. Use forks and other objects, such as cookie stamps, to create patterns and designs on the medallion. For a lacy look, cut shapes completely through

the dough. For an engraved look, do not press your designs deeply into the dough.

7. When you and your child have finished designing the medallions, carefully lift the foil and the medallions onto the cookie sheet. Wrap any leftover dough in plastic wrap. The Salt Dough will not stay moist for more than a few days.

8. Bake the medallions for several hours at 200°F (95°C) until they are completely dry. The dough will also dry at room temperature in 3 to 5 days.

9. Allow the salt dough medallions to cool. Then remove the foil from the back of the baked medallions. Glue beads, glitter, and other decorations into place, if your child wishes.

10. Pull ribbon or string through the top hole, and knot it. Your child can wear her medallion or use it as a wall plaque.

☆ ☆ ☆ ☆   ☆ ☆

MORE IDEAS

•Make Christmas tree decorations by rolling out the Salt Dough and cutting shapes from holiday cookie cutters.

•Sprinkle small amounts of glitter randomly on the unbaked objects, then press them lightly so that the glitter will stick to the dough as it bakes.

•Make small, freestanding figurines. Perhaps you can craft a miniature crèche (manger scene) to display at Christmastime or sparkly little angels to adorn a holiday buffet table.

Recipe File

DOUGHS, PAINTS, INKS & POTPOURRI

Ingredients
- 4 cups (920 g) of flour
- 1 cup (230 g) of salt
- 1½ cups (360 ml) of water

Flour Dough

This dough is very pliable, and it rarely cracks when drying. Flour Dough can be braided, pressed through a garlic press, molded, and rolled—all with good results. The dough will, however, puff slightly while baking, which can provide interesting effects. To make a colorful object, use food coloring or natural dyes before modeling. Or simply apply acrylic paints after drying. All objects made from Flour Dough, such as the Mouse in a Cradle project (see page 72), should be sealed when dry so that they will last. It's best to use clear acrylic spray, shellac, or varnish.

DIRECTIONS hot

1. Stir all the ingredients in a large mixing bowl.
2. Place the dough on a floured surface, and knead until it becomes smooth. If the dough is too stiff, add more water, a little at a time.

3. Store unused Flour Dough in a plastic bag in the refrigerator. It should keep indefinitely, but you may need to add more flour with each use.

4. To bake Flour Dough objects, place them on a foil-covered cookie sheet, and bake them at 300°F (150°C) until they're dry and hard. It will take 2 to 4 hours, depending on the object(s) that you're baking.

NOTE: Keep an eye on your baking. Overdried objects will tend to be more fragile, and colors will not be as bright as those perfectly baked. Underbaked projects, on the other hand, will not keep well.

Salt Dough

Ingredients
- 2 cups (460 g) of salt
- ⅔ cup (160 ml) of water
- 1 cup (230 g) of cornstarch
- ½ cup (120 ml) of cold water
- Aluminum foil
- Cookie sheets

This dough is heavy and very white, with a sparkling, shimmering look. It is used in the Mouse in a Cradle project (see page 72) and Mosaic Medallions (see page 108). Salt Dough can dry effectively at room temperature or in a warm oven. The finished dough projects will be extremely hard and durable when dry. To make a colorful project, work food coloring, natural dyes, or water-based paint into the dough before modeling. Coloring Salt Dough creations after they dry will make the dough dull, instead of having its usual sparkle.

DIRECTIONS hot

CAUTION: Steps 1 and 3 require cooking over a hot stove. It is recommended that you do these steps rather than your child.

1. Stir ⅔ cup (160 ml) of water and all the salt together in a saucepan over medium heat until it is well heated. Remove the pan from the stove.

2. Mix ½ cup (120 ml) of cold water and all the cornstarch together. Add the cornstarch mixture slowly to the salt mixture.

3. Return the pan to the stove, and cook the dough over medium heat until the mixture forms a soft ball. Remove the pan from the stove.

4. Put the dough on a foil-covered cookie sheet, and cover it with a damp cloth until it cools.

5. Shape objects on a foil-covered cookie sheet.

6. To dry Salt Dough objects, bake them in an oven at 200°F (95°C) for several hours. Or allow them to air-dry for 2 to 3 days.

Cornstarch Clay

Ingredients
- 2 cups (460 g) of baking soda
- 1 cup (230 g) of cornstarch
- 1 ¼ cups (300 ml) of cold water

This modeling clay works well for rolling-pin projects and small sculpted figures (see Mouse in a Cradle, page 72, and Clay Dolls, page 87). It is easy to make and work with, but the clay will crack if it is overdried. So, be careful that you do not bake it too long. You can color the snow-white clay with food coloring or natural dyes before modeling, or use acrylic pains after the objects dry thoroughly.

DIRECTIONS hot

CAUTION: Steps 1 and 2 require cooking over a hot stove. It is recommended that you do these steps rather than your child.

1. In a 2-quart (2l) saucepan, over low heat, mix baking soda and cornstarch. Add the water slowly while stirring to prevent lumps.

2. Cook the mixture for 6 minutes or until it looks like mashed potatoes.

3. To cool, spread the dough on a cookie sheet, and cover it with a damp cloth.

4. Knead the dough for 10 minutes.

5. Store the clay dough in an airtight container when you're not using it. Bake Cornstarch Clay objects at 200°F (95°C) for 1 ½ to 3 hours. Cool and dry your creations completely—for at least 24 hours.

Ingredients
- 2 to 4 cups (460 to 920 g) of soap flakes
- ½ to 1 cup (120 to 240 ml) of water
- Electric mixer

Soap Snow

It's fun to use Soap Snow to make snow sculptures, miniature snow forts, and indoor snowmen and snowwomen (see page 64), but you can also create useful and decorative gift soaps with the same recipe.

DIRECTIONS

1. Begin with 2 cups (460 g) of soap flakes and ½ cup (120 ml) of water.

CAUTION: Step 2 requires the use of a sharp instrument. It is recommended that you do these steps rather than your child.

2. Use an electric mixer to whip the mixture until the "snow" becomes the consistency of cookie dough.

3. Add more flakes and water, as needed.

GIFT SOAPS

To make gift soaps, you can sculpt interesting shapes, then let the Soap Snow item dry completely. If you use cookie cutters, pat the Soap Snow into a thick "sheet" (like rolled cookie dough) on waxed paper or plastic wrap. Then cut out the shapes and allow them to dry. You can also press Soap Snow into candy and cookie molds, then turn onto a surface covered with waxed paper to dry. When the soaps are completely dry, wrap Soap Snow gift soaps individually in tissue paper or plastic wrap.

Ingredients

- 1 stick (8 table-spoons or 114 g) of butter or margarine
- ½ cup (115 g) of sugar
- 2 eggs
- 1 teaspoon (5 ml) of vanilla
- ½ teaspoon (2½ ml) of almond flavoring (optional)
- 2 teaspoons (10 ml) of baking powder
- 2½ cups (575 g) of flour

Sugar Cookies

This unbaked dough can be used for Lollipop Cookies (see page 56).

DIRECTIONS

1. Blend the margarine and sugar until the mixture becomes light and fluffy. If you wish, you can use an electric mixer while your child watches.

2. Add the eggs, vanilla, and almond flavoring. Beat well.

3. Add the baking powder and flour, and mix until the dough forms a ball. The dough will be very stiff.

4. Wrap the dough in plastic, and refrigerate it at least 1 hour before rolling and cutting or shaping it.

5. Roll out the dough to ¼ inch (0.6 cm) thick. Use cookie cutters or form the dough into desired shapes.

6. With a spatula, place the cookies on a greased cookie sheet. Bake in a preheated oven at 350°F (175°C) for 10 to 12 minutes, or until done.

MORE IDEAS

With this basic recipe, you and your child can invent many cookie variations. Make Lollipop Cookies topped with a frosting glaze, or add nuts, chocolate chips, or gumdrops. Experiment to see what suits both of your taste buds.

Ingredients

- ½ cup (115 g) of shortening
- 1 cup (230 g) of sugar
- 1 egg
- ¾ cup (180 ml) of milk
- 1 teaspoon (5 ml) of vanilla
- 1¾ cups (402 g) of flour
- ½ cup (115 g) of unsweetened cocoa powder
- ½ teaspoon (2½ ml) of baking soda
- ½ teaspoon (2½ g) of salt
- Electric mixer
- Popsicle sticks
- Baking sheet
- Spatula

For Decoration

- 1 cup (230 g) of chocolate chips
- Colored candy sprinkles

Chocolate Drop Pops

These yummy chocolate drop pops can used as an alternate ingredient for the Lollipop Cookies (see page 56).

DIRECTIONS

CAUTION: Steps 1 and 2 require the use of a sharp instrument. It is recommended that you do these steps rather than your child.

1. With a mixer, blend the shortening, sugar, and egg until creamy. Add milk and vanilla, and beat well.

2. Stir together the flour, cocoa, baking soda, and salt; then beat into the sugar and shortening mixture until the dough is smooth. Drop a heaping teaspoon of dough onto a lightly greased cookie sheet.

3. Place a clean Popsicle stick in the middle of the dropped dough, pressing the stick lightly into the middle, but not all the way to the bottom, of the cookie sheet.

4. Place a small glob of dough on top of the exposed Popsicle stick.

5. Repeat this process until the dough is gone, leaving plenty of space between

each cookie. Eight cookies and sticks fit nicely on an average-size baking sheet.

6. Bake in preheated oven at 350°F (175°C) for 8 to 12 minutes, until done.

7. Cool, and remove the cookies from the pan carefully with a spatula.

TO DECORATE

1. Place 1 cup (230 g) of chocolate chips in a microwavable bowl, and microwave on HIGH for 1 to 3 minutes. Stop the microwave and check the chocolate in order not to over-cook it. Stir frequently.

2. When the chips are just melted, let your child drizzle the chip frosting with a spoon onto the top of the cookie pop, then sprinkle the cookie with colored candy sprinkles.

Ingredients

- 2 tablespoons (28 g) of butter or margarine
- 1½ cups (345 g) of confectioners' sugar
- 1 to 3 table-spoons (15 to 45 ml) of milk
- 1 teaspoon (5 ml) of vanilla extract
- ½ teaspoon (2½ ml) of almond extract

Fast & Fabulous Frosting Glaze

This delicious stuff is not as thick as frosting or as runny as a glaze. It's easy for you and your child to use for the Lollipop Cookies (see page 56).

DIRECTIONS hot

1. Melt the butter and place it in a small bowl. Add the confectioners' sugar and blend. Add the milk to the sugar, 1 tablespoon (15 ml) at a time, beating until the frosting is thick enough to drop slowly from a spoon. Add the vanilla and almond extracts and beat well.

2. When you use the frosting glaze, a thin "crust" may form on the top. Stir the frosting regularly in the bowl while you are applying it.

Crunchy Creature Stew

Since Crunchy Creature Stew is quite sticky, you can smear it directly onto tree trunks, branches, and stumps as well as use it for the Pinecone Creature Feeders craft (see page 68). All kinds of winged and four-footed creatures will invite themselves to dine in your yard.

Ingredients

- 1 cup (230 g) of peanut butter
- 1 to 2 cups (230 to 460 g) of sunflower seeds or wild birdseed
- ½ cup (115 g) of raisins or cranberries (optional)
- ½ cup (115 g) of peanuts or other nuts (optional)

DIRECTIONS **hot**

CAUTION: Step 1 requires working on a hot surface. It is recommended that you do this step rather than your child.

1. Melt the peanut butter in a large bowl in a microwave, or melt it slowly in a pan on the stove. Remove the pan from the heat, and stir in the rest of the ingredients until they're coated with peanut butter.

2. Adding different ingredients to the basic stew recipe will attract a variety of wild creatures. Bits of bacon or suet will attract woodpeckers. Finches and other songbirds favor thistle seed. Chickadees, jays, and squirrels love peanuts and walnuts.

Natural Dyes & Inks

In early times, people used berries, leaves, roots, and herbs to add color to various everyday objects. They also used these natural objects to paint both face and body. It is *not* a good idea to let your child apply the natural dye on himself because it can be harmful to the skin. But the two of you will have fun making your own paints and inks for drawings and other painted objects from things found in nature. These finished colors may not be as bright as many store-bought products colored with synthetic chemicals, but why not experiment? The both of you can work with color just as ancient peoples once did as you make the Carrot Roller (see page 26), Block Printing (see page 51), and Eggshell Art (see page 53) crafts.

CAUTION: Wear gloves when making natural dyes and inks. It can stain or even irritate the skin.

NATURAL OBJECTS THAT STAIN

Berries: Berries offer a variety of color possibilities. Gather them from fields and forests or buy them from the grocery store. Try raspberries, blueberries, blackberries, and a wide assortment of inedible berries.

Leaves and Grasses: The kind of leaf or grass you collect will determine the color of your dye. Thick green leaves will produce more vivid colors than thinner leaves. However, freshly cut grass works well, too.

Kitchen Spices: Try cinnamon sticks, powdered cinnamon, and gingerroot.

Flower Petals: Blossoms from dandelions, zinnias, daylilies, and tulips are good choices for making dyes, and the colors created from begonia blossoms are especially vibrant.

Tree Bark: Experiment with barks from different trees to discover subtle differences in the colors produced.

Thick Tree Roots and Dried Bulbs: The roots of dead trees and dried flower bulbs create unusual colors, depending on the type of tree or bulb used. These colors will not be bright, but they will produce authentic colors used long ago.

Vegetables and Vegetable Skins: Many vegetables, like carrots, beets, and spinach, which you may have in your home garden or find at the grocery store, make lovely ink and dye colors. The peels from potatoes, zucchini, and onions are just a few of the kinds of vegetable skin which produce natural colors.

DIRECTIONS

CAUTION: Since making dyes require cutting the natural objects and then boiling them, it is recommend that you do these steps rather than your child.

1. Chop all your berries, leaves, grasses, or other natural objects as finely as possible, and place them in a saucepan for the stove or in a glass or ceramic bowl for the microwave.
2. Add enough water to completely cover the objects.
3. On the stove, bring the water to a boil in the saucepan, then allow it to simmer for 15 to 30 minutes. If necessary, add more water, a little at a time. If you use a microwave, heat the items in the bowl on high for 3 to 8 minutes—until the water turns into the color you want.
4. Cooking times will vary, depending on the number and quality of the items you are using. Experiment with cooking time, amount of water, and the number of natural objects used for dyes to produce the effect you desire. Trial and error is how our ancient forebears learned, too!
5. Don't expect natural inks and dyes to be as vivid as synthetic inks and dyes. To produce brighter natural colors, increase the amount of petals, roots, leaves, berries, blossoms, bark, skins, grounds, grasses, or vegetables, and combine them with a small amount of water. Cook slowly for a longer period, stirring frequently.

CREATING SPECIFIC COLORS

Brown: Roots, bark, coffee grounds, tea bags.

Red: Cranberries, beets, raspberries, bright-red wild berries.

Blue: Blueberries, chopped red cabbage, red onion skins.

Green: Grass clippings, green leaves, parsley, spinach, moss.

Yellow: Flower blossoms such as yellow marigolds and daffodils, yellow onion skins.

Purple: Blackberries, purple plums, purple flower blossoms.

Orange: Combine yellow and red dyes, or use carrots.

USES FOR NATURAL DYES

•Dye fabrics and yarns.

•Stain everyday objects.

•Use them as a substitute for watercolor paints.

•Dye eggshells (see Eggshell Art, page 53). Only use dyes made from *edible* substances if you plan to eat the eggs inside.

•Create stamping ink (see Roller Printing, page 25, and Block Printing, page 51).

•Color homemade craft doughs like the Salt Dough (see page 114), Flour Dough (see page 112), or Cornstarch Clay (see page 116).

Stamp Pads

You can buy ink-filled stamp pads from craft, variety, and office supply stores. These pads will work well with your own roller printers (see page 25) and with small, handmade printing blocks (see page 51). You and your child can also make your own stamp pads. It's fairly easy.

You'll Need
- Small sponge for each color
- Container slightly larger than the sponge with a tightly fitting lid
- Paint, bottled ink, or natural dye

DIRECTIONS

Place the sponge in the container bowl, and saturate it with the colored paint, ink, or dye. Avoid oversaturating the pad, or you'll just get a puddle in the bottom of the bowl. In fact, if the sponge is not very wet, the printer will work better, and the paper on which you print will dry more quickly.

When the stamp pad is not in use, secure the container's lid, and store it in a cool place. If you use natural materials for the dye, store the pad in the refrigerator to reduce mold growth. If you do not use the ink pad for a long time, you may need to add a few drops of water or paint to the sponge to make it wet once more.

About Paints & Inks

Acrylics: Acrylic paints work well on porous surfaces, like things made out of doughs and clays. You'll find acrylics in tubes and jars in variety stores and craft shops. It's OK to thin these paints with water for watercolor painting, but they work best on homemade crafts when you add little or no water.

Fabric Paints: There is a wide variety of paints available in craft and sewing stores which work well with fabrics. Some of these fabric paints come in tubes or bottles with narrow tips for writing words and making fine line designs. Others are specifically for splatter-painting or tie-dyeing. You'll find sparkly paints and glow-in-the-dark paints, too. And the best thing about many of these products is they are easy to use and machine-washable.

If you want to get creative with these paints, you and your child can smear the colors on your fabric using small pieces of cardboard as "paintbrushes." Or dip cardboard shapes into some squeezed-out paint and press onto the fabric. Lift carefully to prevent smearing the design.

Let painted items dry flat for 12 to 24 hours before using. And wait at least 3 days before laundering. Machine drying is not recommended.

Food Coloring: Mix 1 teaspoon (5 ml) of vinegar for each ½ cup (120 ml) of water, and food coloring will perform as a dye. But be careful: colors can bleed and fade when laundered. Also try food coloring for printing with blocks and rollers (see pages 25 and 51).

Ink: Bottled ink is available in a variety of colors. You can buy it at office supply or variety stores. Use these inks for painting nonporous surfaces as well as for block and roller printing (see pages 25 and 51). You can also find ready-to-use stamp pads in many colors. Also look for rainbow stamp pads that include several colors in a single pad.

Natural Dyes and Paints: Made from substances found in nature, these dyes and paints provide unusual color options for craft projects. Most colors created from natural materials will not turn out as vivid as synthetic colors. However, these dyes offer subtle tones, and they allow for lots of creativity.

Tempera: This water-based paint can be used wherever watercolors might be used. Tempera comes in powdered form as well as liquid form, and is available in variety, craft, and art stores.

Watercolors: Watercolor paints are available in most stores, and they're inexpensive. They work best on less porous surfaces. Avoid using them on most homemade dough creations, since the moisture will soften the finished product. When mixed with small amounts of water, watercolors can be used to color eggshells (see page 53). But use them only if you remove the egg before coloring.

Potpourri

Potpourri can be put in Burlap Baskets (see page 100) or jars as air fresheners, or stuffed into tiny pillows for sachets. Sachets add a nice fragrance to closets and drawers—and to the clothes kept inside. Experiment with your child using a variety of flowers, spices, and oils to find the scents both of you will like. Most of the ingredients for potpourris can be found in the spice section of grocery stores, in craft shops, in your own kitchen, and in backyard gardens.

DIRECTIONS

1. Choose one or more ingredient from *each* of the four groups above: bases, spices, oils, and fixative. Let your noses decide which fragrances blend nicely.
2. Dry the flower petals and citrus peels. Place them in single layers on paper towels and allow them to air-dry, which may take from several days to weeks.

Suggested Ingredients

Bases
- Rose petals
- Lavender blossoms
- Peppermint leaves
- Geranium petals
- Peel from lemons, limes, oranges, and tangerines

Fixative
- Orrisroot

Spices
- Allspice
- Cinnamon
- Nutmeg
- Cloves
- Ginger
- Mace

Oils
- Lemon and orange oils
- Rose oil
- Perfume

Or place the petals and peels in a single layer on paper towels and process them in a microwave oven for 3 to 5 minutes on medium. If you air-dry the petals and peels, replace the paper towels daily. Turn the petals and peels over to speed their drying and prevent them from becoming moldy. For your potpourri, these petals and peels should be *very* dry, like brown fall leaves that easily crumble.

3. In a large bowl, mix several cups of the flower petals or citrus peels, 1 to 2 tablespoons (14 to 28 ml) of each of your chosen spices, 6 to 10 drops of *one* oil, and 2 teaspoons (9 g) of orrisroot.

Your potpourri is ready to use.

Acknowledgments

Many of the projects presented in this book were inspired by friends and teachers I've worked with either as a child and as an adult. Thanks to all of you for sharing your creativity with me and helping me to take flight on my own creative wings.

Special thanks to Sterling Publishing for believing in this book and making it happen.

Most of all, thanks to the parents who purchase this book and use it with their child to create, laugh, and learn together. May you find much enjoyment as you explore these pages.

About the Author

Judith Logan Lehne lives in a log home deep in the woods of Wisconsin with her husband, Kent, their dogs, Kelly and Clancy, and a wide assortment of occasional guests, including whitetail deer, black bear, and coyotes. Judi has four children, Shane, Kyle, Todd, and Tessa, two stepchildren, Kristofer and Kirsten, and two grandchildren, Brendan and Elijah.

Over seventy of Judi's stories and articles have appeared in magazines for children and adults. Five of her plays have been produced. She has also been a recipient of the *Highlights for Children* Outstanding Author award.

Her first novel, *When the Ragman Sings* (HarperCollins, 1993), was a Pick of the List by American Bookseller Association. *Coyote Girl* (Simon & Schuster, 1995) received high praise by reviewers and young readers, and *Kangaroos for Kids* (NorthWord Press, 1997) was a long-standing Recommended Book by *Ranger Rick* magazine. Judi's works of fiction and nonfiction have also been included in several anthologies and educational materials.

In addition to her writing, Judi is a coordinator and advocate for persons with severe mental illness. She conducts multi-creative and writing workshops for children and adults, and is an instructor for The Institute of Children's Literature. In her free time, she enjoys sculpting, crafting, skiing, snorkeling, reading, traveling, and music.

Index